Writing to Respond

CULTIVATING A HABIT

Martha Joseph Watts

Print information available on the last page

Rev. date: 08/29/2018

To order additional copies of this book, contact:
Xlibris
1-888-795-4274
www.Xlibris.com
Orders@Xlibris.com

CONTENTS

Reviews

Martha Joseph Watts' new book, *Writing to Respond: Cultivating a Habit,* is an answer to each teacher's/parent's cry for help. This five-step process is "aimed at cultivating a habit of writing in students through structure and practice." As a teacher of writing, I eagerly embrace this book as it engages students in writing and critical thinking. It requires students to become actively engaged with the text by asking them to respond with their ideas and experiences and by using "new words," thus enhancing their vocabulary.

This student-friendly text empowers students by inviting them to express their reactions, thus forcing them to entertain opposing views while applying principles of argumentation. It also asks for students' suggestions, and questions. By assuring students that their ideas are theirs, and are not "right or wrong," Joseph Watts guides students in the process of owning their writing, and simultaneously, owning the text.

Writing to Respond: Cultivating a Habit is a student friendly, nonthreatening process that engages students while teaching them MLA and APA styles of documentation. It also introduces them to the writer's journal, a tool that will prove beneficial to students in their academic experiences and beyond. The fact that Joseph Watts has actually used this process and has involved her colleagues in experimenting with it in their classes is a powerful testimony to its practicality and relevance in education. There is no doubt in my mind that this process will revolutionize writing and critical thinking, not only in the Virgin Islands, but among all students who are exposed to the process.

Valerie Knowles Combie, Ph.D.
Associate Professor,
College of Liberal Arts and Social Sciences, UVI
Director, Virgin Islands Writing Project (VIWP)

Dedication

This directional guide is dedicated
To my nieces and nephews, students, teachers
and schools everywhere.

It is specifically dedicated to schools that continue to provide
opportunities to enhance student learning
through magazine subscription.

To the students whom I have been privileged to teach

To the desire of my mother that
ALL children read and write well.

Acknowledgement

Thanks

To Almighty God for Favor

To the Chicken Hawk Family at the Charlotte Amalie
High School where this project was birthed.

To the students for embracing it;
To the teachers for utilizing it, and to the
Administrators for recognizing it

To the Virgin Islands Writing Project (VIWP)
for stirring dormant ideas, and

Special thanks

To my husband, George Watts for his support,
my son Vaughn Registe for his artistic input, to my family,
colleagues, and to all those around me who recognized my
potential and persuaded me insensately

A Note to Parents and Teachers

Writing to Respond is a five step process aimed at cultivating a habit of writing in students through structure and practice. Although the steps focus on responding to an "article", the intention is that students will be able to transfer skills acquired from one form of literature to another.

This style is meant to encourage students to interact with informational text. If used consistently, it will also motivate reluctant students to orally express their reactions and will build their confidence both in oral and written expression.

This format allows for feedback without the added pressure of using the colored pen. The aim is to create an avenue for writing that is non-threatening, and to reward students for being consistent with responses and displaying evidence of progress overtime.

Teachers, parents, give students ownership. Let them write at home or in-class. Give them an opportunity to be responsible for their progress and reward them for their efforts.

If we provide clear and systematic instructions, good examples, fair opportunities for practice, easy to use rubrics, and a time to share, more students will be successful. This project attempts to help teachers and parents guide students through this process of developing a successful writing habit.

This concept has been utilized with students in English and Business classes at Charlotte Amalie High School for the past three years, and there is evidence to suggest that it contributes to building students' confidence in oral and written communication. Try it. It works.

A Note to Students

Dear students,

Think of the many times your teachers have asked you to write a report, a review or a response and your first question was, "How?"

This was the exact reaction of my 10th-grade students three years ago when I asked them to respond to an article form a *Scholastic Action* magazine.

I realized that I had to do more than tell. I had to provide a map—a map that students could keep in their folders or staple to their copy books.

My students read, wrote, and pleaded to share their work. Their eagerness convinced me that other students could benefit from this map. Since then, I have shared it with many other students and teachers, and the results have been awe inspiring.

This is why I am sharing this map with you and students everywhere. You deserve to read, write, and share without the intimidation of your teacher's colored pen or demanding tone. Have fun. Read! Write! Share!

Purpose

To cultivate a habit of writing

Objectives

Writing *to Respond to an Article* will help you:

- Read with purpose
- Interact with what you read
- Write your reactions to what you read
- Use transitions to combine sentences
- Write proper citations for specific sources
- Identify your errors in grammar and sentence structure
- Engage in class discussions

With constant practice and use of this guide, you will:

- Develop an appreciation for informational text
- Become more comfortable with writing
- Use the same skills to respond to other forms of literature
- Be more conscious about your errors in grammar.—
- Become more competent in expressing your feelings—
- Become knowledgeable in the use of in-text citations

Here's How

Name the article, author and the publication

☞ Identify the title. It is usually located at the top of the article and the words are usually written in larger print than the other words in the article.

☞ If there is an author, the name will appear just below the title before the start of the story. If there is no author, that's fine.

☞ Write the date the article was published, and the name of the magazine in which it was published.

You might ask why this is important, but this is how your readers can locate the article if they would like to read it.

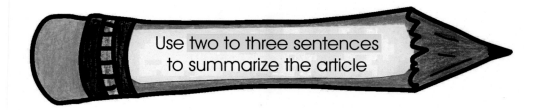
Use two to three sentences to summarize the article

☞ Give an idea of what the article is about without retelling the entire story, and without leaving out the most important aspects of the article.

☞ To achieve this goal it is a good idea to mark important ideas as you read. At the end of the summary, always place your in-text citation. If you join this section to the one before, you will only need a page number. However, if you write individual paragraphs for each section, you will need to include the author's last name and the page number at end of the last sentence of your summary. If there is no author, place a shortened title of the article in quotation marks along with a page number.

This simply means you are acknowledging that you did not make up this information. You read it somewhere.

Although this example follows Modern Language Association (MLA) format, you can use resources available to you to find out the correct method for other formats.

Please note, MLA format uses present tense to respond to literature.

Your summary might be longer depending on your grade level, personal taste or length of the article.

React to what you read

☞ It would be extremely boring to your audience if you just picked an article and retell it. This is your moment to invite your audience to experience your reaction. Are you surprised, happy, amazed, puzzled or upset? Tell your readers.

☞ Connect the situation to something you know. If you remember a similar event, this is a good time to link what you already know to the new information.

☞ This is also a fine opportunity to use new words to express your feelings about what you've read. Use a thesaurus to help you. Although your audience might not always agree with your reactions, that's ok. These are your feelings presented in a non-offensive manner.

What questions do you have?

☞ Somehow, authors always leave some unanswered questions, or they write about issues that pose questions. Many times other readers are able to help clear up these questions, but there are times you may have to do some research or find out from the author.

Meanwhile, here is a place to ask your questions. Write them down. You can seek help later.

What suggestions do you have?

☞ At this juncture, you can make suggestions. Your suggestions can be directed to the author, the magazine, or to your readers. If the article presented a problem, give suggestions on how the problem should be solved.
☞ These are your thoughts. They are not right or wrong. Your audience can disagree, but must respect your ideas.

You are now on your own

☞ At first, you will write your responses under each heading. You will then use transition words and phrases to combine your sentences into a paragraph.

☞ Start simple. Use coordinating conjunctions. As you become more confident, use transitional phrases.

☞ Once you've grasped the idea, you can move straight into paragraph writing. Be creative. Write with style. The key is to have all five aspects in every response.

Examine the example below before you begin. You will notice slight differences between the sentences and the paragraph. This is because the writer may choose to use different words to improve flow and style.

Let's take a look at an example

Name the article, author and publication.

The article "Star Stage" is presented in the February 1, 2010 issue of the *Scholastic Action magazine.*

Use two to three sentences to summarize the article.

Be sure to cite your source

The article announces that the Apollo Theater in Harlem, New York city is celebrating 75 years. It also highlights the idea that the theater contributed to the success of many African-American artists ("Star Stage" 3).

React to what you read

Write your feelings about it. Do you agree or disagree? Are you surprised or sad? Connect the situation to what you already know.

Wow! That's cool. It means that Apollo provided great opportunities for African American who probably would not have otherwise gotten opportunities to become famous.

What questions do you have?

What if the Apollo was never created? Would African-Americans like Michael Jackson become so famous?

What suggestions do you have?

I think that other states and territories should mimic the actions of New York City and create avenues for individuals with talent to better their chances of becoming famous.

Once you've understood the structure, you can add a creative edge to your writing. Be sure to write the final version in paragraph form.

Opportunities to Shine

The article "Star Stage" is presented in the February 1, 2010 issue of the *Scholastic Action magazine*. It announces that the Apollo Theater in Harlem, New York city is celebrating 75 years, **and** states that the theater contributed to the success of many African-American artists (3). Wow! I think that's very fortunate. **Therefore**, this means that Apollo provided great opportunities for African-Americans who probably would not have otherwise **obtained** opportunities to become famous. What if the Apollo was never created? Would African-Americans like Michael Jackson have become so famous?. **Because of this great success**, I think other states and territories should mimic the actions of New York City **by providing avenues** for individuals with talent to shine.

Your Turn

Find an article. Read and write to respond to it. Use the checklist below to check your progress.

Time to check your work.

Give yourself one ☑ if you can answer YES at the end of each aspect.

- ☑ I have identified the title of the article. I have stated the name of the magazine, and the date of publication. I have also acknowledged the author.
- ☑ I have summarized the article. I included important information, but I did not retell the story. I have used proper in-text citation.
- ☑ I have written reactions to what I read. I have made connections to situations I know about.
- ☑ I have asked questions of the author or about the issue.
- ☑ I have made at least one suggestion.

If you have responded satisfactorily to all aspects you will earn a 5/5.

- ☞ When you read your work out loud to a peer, a parent, or to your class, you will hear your errors in grammar. Take some time to correct these errors.
- ☞ Feel free to re-write or just improve on your next response.

As you practice responding to articles you will become more confident, and you will be able to respond to other forms of literature.

Here is your writing Affirmation

I can write

I will Write

I am writing

Student Sample

Student Sample 1 by Anthony Etienne Jr

Following Dreams

The article" Hawk Still Soaring" is presented in the March 8, 2010 issue of the Scholastic Scope magazine. The article is written by Jennifer Dignan in the form of a vocabulary exercise. It announces that as a child, Tony Hawk found skateboarding to be a perfect way to channel his energy. With practice and a lot of work, by age 16, he was known as the best skater in the world (23).

That's a great achievement! Hank's experience shows me that with hard work, I can do anything I set my mind to. What if Tony Hawk had given up when he had gotten hurt during his skateboarding practices? Would skateboarding be as famous as it is today? Because of what Hank was able to achieve, I think that other young people should never give up when they encounter difficulties. They should follow their dreams regardless of their challenges. .

Student Sample 2 by Elisha John Baptiste

Sneaking Food

The article I read is titled, "Is it OK to Sneak Food into the Movies". It is presented in the May 14, 2012 issue of the Scholastic Scope and the author is Justin O'Neil. It presents the different views that people share about the problem of sneaking food in the movie theater. Sneaking food is against the theater rules and if caught the person can be kicked out or banned from the theater. But some people think that the snacks sold at the theater are very expensive, so they bring their own food. They even bring smelly foods like tuna sandwich (28).

OMG (Oh my gosh!) This is crazy. If movie goers are planning to sneak food, they should at least bring foods that do not have a bad smell like candies and snack bars. How do they pass with food and not get caught? Sneaking food in a theatre is a bad habit, but I think if someone really has to sneak food into the movie, then it should be something that is small and does not have a smell.

Other sample

Endangered

I read the article titled, "Tiny P.R. Frog gets Federal Protection" in the Caribbean section of the Friday October 5, 2012 issue of The Virgin Islands Daily News. The article states that a small tree frog in Puerto Rico has been classified as an endangered species. This means that it will be against the law to kill that frog because there are not many of them left on the Island (8).

I have heard about other animals in the Caribbean being protected because people capture them for use as pets; or kill them for food. The Sisserou Parrot, the Leather Back Turtle, and some snakes are examples of other endangered species in the Caribbean. There are endangered species all over the world. Even some plants are protected by law. Why would people want to kill off or make an animal or plant become extinct? Is that what happened to the dinosaurs?

I think it is a great idea to punish people for not being more concerned about protecting animals that are rare. I suggest that students also learn about the importance of protecting animals.

Challenge

Now that you are good at responding to articles, try the following to strengthen your writing skills.

- ➤ Conduct research to find out more about an article or issue that evoked more questions than answers.
- ➤ Write a synthesis essay on one of the controversial views.
- ➤ Write an argumentative essay on one of the debatable views.
- ➤ Write a letter to an author or the editor of a magazine.
- ➤ Create a project in reaction to one of the articles or issues you care about.
- ➤ Respond to other types of literature a story, movie, play, TV news report, newspaper article, or an advertisement

Works Cited

The Associated Press, "Tiny P.R. Frog gets Federal Protection" *The Virgin Islands Daily News,* 5 Oct: 20012: 8. Print

Dignan, Jennifer. "Hawk Still Soaring" *Scholastic Scope,*.8 March 2010: 23. Print

Modern Language Association. *The MLA Handbook for Writers of Research Papers,* 7th ed. New York: Modern Language Association, 2009. Print.

O Niel, Justin, " Is it Okay to Sneak Food into the Movies" Scholastic Scope, 14 May 2012:28. Print.

"Star Stage". *Scholastic Action,* 1 Feb. 2010: 3. Print.

My

Journal

Students work used with parental consent.

Anthony Etienne Jr, Grade 6 , Virgin Islands School District.
Elisha John Baptiste, Grade 5 , Virgin Islands School District.

Vaughn K Registe, illustrator, is a 2007 graduate of Charlotte Amalie High School, and 2012 of Florida Career College. He aspires to pursue his dream as an illustrator/graphic designer.

About The Author

Martha is a graduate of the Dominica Teachers Training College, (1998) and the University of the Virgin Islands (2002, 2005). She is a recipient of the Virgin Islands Humanities Council's Heath Award (2010). She has served as an elementary teacher, and currently serves as an English teacher at Charlotte Amalie High school and as adjunct writing instructor at the University of the Virgin Islands.

Martha is an active member of the Virgin Islands Writing Project (2003). She has presented to parents and teachers on the topic of children and non-fiction writing in conferences with *Kids Count* and the Virgin Island Writing Project (VIWP). She continues to present in conferences on matters of literacy with the VIWP and the Caribbean Studies Association (CSA).

Martha attends the St. Thomas Assembly of God where she serves in the Sunday school and Prison Ministries. She is married to George Watts and, has a son, Vaughn Registe.

Look for other topics on Children and Non-Fiction Writing from Martha Joseph Watts.

Printed in the United States
By Bookmasters